# HOW TO START A MENTAL HEALTH PRIVATE PRACTICE

## BUILD YOUR PRACTICE AND DOUBLE YOUR PAYCHECK IN 4 SIMPLE STEPS

JESSICA M. MILLER, M.A.

Simple Press

Simple Press
New Prague, Minnesota 56071
simplepressbooks.com

**How to Start a Mental Health Private Practice,**
Build your practice and DOUBLE YOUR PAYCHECK in
4 SIMPLE STEPS



Cover & Interior Design: Sel P

Editor: Scribendi

**Print ISBN: 978-0-9963093-0-1**

**ePub ebook ISBN: 978-0-9963093-1-8**

**Kindle ebook ISBN: 978-0-9963093-2-5**

1. Practice Management. 2. Psychotherapy–organization and administration. 3. Counseling–organization and administrations. 4. Marketing of Health Services

Printed in United States

10 9 8 7 6 5 4 3 2 1

# TABLE OF CONTENTS

Introduction: My Background ........................................................ 1

Step 1: Research and Development ............................................. 7

*Part 1: Determine the Target Population* ........................................... 9

*Part 2: Develop Your Brand and Create a Mission Statement* ........... 13

*Part 3: Market Saturation and Demand for Services* ........................ 17

Step 2: Ideal Lifestyle and Realistic Budget Planning .................. 23

*Part 1: What Is Your Ideal Lifestyle?* .............................................. 25

*Part 2: How Much Overhead Is Too Much?* .................................... 29

*Part 3: Manage Risks* ..................................................................... 39

Step 3: Building a Solid Infrastructure ........................................ 47

*Part 1: Making Your Practice Legitimate* ........................................ 49

*Part 2: Creating Documents and Forms* .......................................... 53

*Part 3: Building a Website* .............................................................. 57

*Part 4: Choosing an Electronic Health Records (EHRs) Platform* ..... 61

*Part 5: Opting for Fee-for-Service or Insurance-Based Practice* ......... 63

Step 4: Spreading the News! ..... 71

*Part 1: How to Reach Your Target Market* ..... 73

*Part 2: Introduction to Pay-per-Click Advertising* ..... 77

Bonus Materials: Expanding Your Practice, Earning Passive Income, and Paying it Forward ..... 81

*Part 3: Expanding Your Practice* ..... 83

*Part 4: Earning Passive Income* ..... 87

*Part 5: Paying It Forward* ..... 91

Closing Thoughts ..... 93

For Further Reading ..... 95

# INTRODUCTION: MY BACKGROUND

I grew up with two entrepreneurs for parents. Together they owned a trucking company. It was mainly a family managed operation, and everyone played a role, including our petite mom, who drove an 18-wheeler. My life in the truck began when I was just three weeks old. From sunrise to sunset, I bounced down the road five to six days a week. While other kids my age were waking up on Saturday mornings to the smell of pancakes and watching cartoons, I would wake to the smell of McDonald's coffee in the driver's cup holder and donuts waiting for me in mine.

When I share with people that I grew up in a semi-truck, I mean it, and I am grateful that I did. I learned the most about owning and operating a business from spending time with my parents and other business professionals. My father was a visionary. He could predict market trends, had the confidence to act on business opportunities, and maintained customer relations like a smooth-talking salesman. I inherited these traits from him. I have the natural ability to either think of a business idea or hear someone present a concept and determine after a few questions if it would be a success or a struggle.

My parents would chat into the night about various business deals, and I had a front-row seat to listen and absorb every moment. At our dinner table, I learned about profit margins, product innovation, and recouping losses. Another business skill I picked up from them was the ability to efficiently construct a cost-benefit analysis on practically any business idea.

Growing up, I remember that my favorite commercial on television featured a caveman hammering a rock with a chisel. The message in the ad was, if you had an idea or invention, call the agency, and the firm would help you make it a reality. I honestly cannot recall a single time that I saw that commercial and found myself at a loss for an idea. I always had something brewing in my mind, even at a very young age. I loved that advertisement, and it's my goal to be like its creators. I want to help you (the caveman) infuse oxygen into your dream and idea (the rock). I firmly believe that anyone can create a successful private practice, and by the end of this book, you will, too.

Throughout high school, I continued to work for my parents; but on the side, I started a cleaning business called Busy Bees (simply because I wanted something of my own). It kept me busy, and I made decent income. When it was time to start college, I ended up handing over my clientele to a friend who had been inspired to start her own cleaning company. Then in college, I decided to go back to my roots and drive a semi-truck to make enough money to graduate debt free. During this period, I ended up getting injured by an animal while unloaded a trailer and could no longer drive a truck. Out of necessity, I started my second business, a small dessert company called Tasty Temptations. This was a big hit! Although it wasn't my passion, I worked full-time until I could return to the truck business, when once again I gave my client list to another entrepreneur in the sweets industry.

During my undergraduate years, I had the opportunity to become more involved in the family business, when at various times my parents experienced serious health problems. During these periods, I was privileged to help close deals and create company brands. I was in charge of marketing, providing for employees, and delivering quality services. This was my first business "high," if you will, and you never forget your first when you are a born entrepreneur. From that period forward, there was no doubt in my mind that at some point in my life, I would be creating, building, and branding companies and products for myself and to help others.

The third business, which I co-founded with my husband Ryan, offers personal training and nutritional services. Similar to any startup, it was slow to get going, yet as time passed, we were able to build a highly respected reputation by producing effective workout/nutritional programs. Today our business has grown exponentially. Ryan wrote a book and now provides online training to clients from all around the world. We are now about to launch a T-shirt company, along with a custom car garage that will continue to expand his brand. We started off investing zero dollars and have now created a company that brings in six-figures in income annually.

While I was in my master's program for marriage and family therapy, I was fortunate enough to land a paid internship (rare opportunity). What made this even more exceptional was that within two months of working there, I convinced the owner of the private practice to open a satellite office in my home town so that I could begin to establish a professional reputation in my own community and be closer to my family and children.

Together, my supervisor and I decided on our overhead, and I did all the groundwork. After considering several locations, I ultimately found one below our budget, and we negotiated a lower payment by signing a longer-term lease agreement. I was in charge of furnishing the entire space and of managing the office as my own, since we split the lease payment.

Throughout my internship, I stayed close to my supervisor's side, watching and learning everything I could about managing a private practice. He is an entrepreneur himself and excels at creating a thriving practice that is mainly fee-for-service in a community surrounded by clinics that accept insurance. I had every intention of staying on with him and hoped to cofound a business together; however, things didn't go the way I'd anticipated. We hit a rough patch where communication sank to an all-time low, and I felt like I was once again working for my parents in high school and had no authority to make any marketing decisions to develop the satellite location. Ultimately, after much discussion with my other supervisor and Ryan, I decided that it was time to open my own practice.

Opening a fourth business was a great opportunity to start something on my own in my field of interest; however, I would be remiss if I didn't tell you that I was scared to take this step. Here I was, freshly graduated with my master's degree, a rookie of a therapist, yet I was considering opening a practice in a town with a population of less than 8,000 people. Additionally, there were all the horror stories from veterans in this field-as I'm sure you have heard-telling me that it couldn't be done without participating on insurance panels. What's more the failure rate of startup practices would make anyone think twice about investing funds.

### *What Helped Me Make My Decision?*

During my time working in private practice, I refined my skills in closing deals (signing on clients). I had a very high client retention rate and began receiving a higher volume of client referrals. This was tremendously reassuring. I also recalled the discussions with my parents around the dinner table, about the cost-benefit analysis process, about the worst-case scenario if I completely failed, and about how I could recoup the loss. In the end, that was all I needed to move forward in opening my very own private practice.

In less than a year, at my practice, South Metro Counseling (SMC), I managed to fill my caseload and that of another clinician, as well as to bring on a second independent contractor (IC), who is on her way to having a full caseload. Currently, SMC is starting Back 2 Good (B2G), a sister company that will allow me to expand the product line and create a larger brand within this industry. We are also negotiating to open a second location, which is expected to launch in the fall of 2015; and we just expanded the original office space. In that same year, I wrote my first book, *Back 2 Love*, which is set for release in the summer of 2015.

When I get an idea for a business, I experience the same thrill that my father did. Planning how I could maximize my gains, limit the risks, and make it a success without selling my soul and giving up a lot of my time is simply euphoric for me. Business is a major passion of mine; that's why I started four of my own, why I am always innovating new ideas, and why I decided to write this book. I believe that if you have a dream for your life, you should surround yourself with others who support your dream, and then figure out a way to make it happen. Buying this book was a first step in actualizing your vision, and I'm honored to be part of it.

My goal in this book is to put as much enthusiasm and passion into the words on the page as I can to simulate what it would be like if you and I were in the same room. I get very excited about business, and I want you to experience that same feeling. This is a grand opportunity that you're about to embark on, and I want you to savor each step along the way. Too often we become almost paralyzed because we don't know which steps to take to realize our dreams. In this book, I streamline the process of opening your very own private practice, simplify the steps of branding your company, and teach you how to market for success. By the end of this short read, you will have gained the confidence in moving forward with your vision and have a plan to proceed from your starting point to your intended destination.

The first step to complete will be research and development. You'll determine what areas of the mental health field you are truly passionate about, want to specialize in, and are drawn towards. These three areas will form the foundation of the brand you will build within the infrastructure of your private practice and help you spend your marketing dollars more wisely.

STEP ONE

# RESEARCH AND DEVELOPMENT

## PART I

# DETERMINE THE TARGET POPULATION

The first step in developing a successful private practice is to determine which populations you are passionate about serving and what areas in the mental health field excite you enough for specialization. In the beginning stages of developing my business plan for SMC, my supervisor and mentor Alan Davis advised me to do the following.

*Pick three areas that you are exceptionally good at.*

Without hesitation, I responded, "couples, teens, and personal growth."

*Now, get really good in those three areas and market specifically to those populations. Get so good that you become known as the practice to go [to] if the client falls into one of those three categories.*

Once you determine your areas of specialization, stay true to your choice. Yes, you can branch out here and there, but if you really want to be effective in one sphere, you need to practice, train, and continue to grow in that specific domain. In my case, it means that if a parent calls in looking for post-traumatic stress disorder (PTSD) treatment for her six-year-old child, I will refer this case to others, because PTSD and children this young are not SMC's focus. To some practitioners, this may seem risky. Others may think that it's counterproductive to narrow down which populations they serve. You may fear that the phone may not ring from a client that meets the specified populations that you treat. You're right; this is a daunting choice to make. You don't know when the phone will ring again, and when times are slow, you'll be tempted to take on any client for whatever type of treatment he or she needs. I remember when SMC first opened, we rode in on a huge wave of clients coming, and then boom, everything stopped, and we hit a three-month standstill without even a single phone call (from our specified clientele). I was fearful. It was my first slow period in my own practice, and I began second guessing my approach, my decision to open, my knowledge about business, and so on. However, through a lot of mentoring from my supervisor and support from Ryan, I managed to make it through the rough summer months and stay true to my brand. You can imagine what happened next: I survived, SMC carried on, and my practice began to grow gradually.

I had turned away several clients before we started building up our caseload that matched the populations in which we wanted to specialize. During this phase, you have to trust the process and know that once your reputation is built and maintained, word spreads fast. Soon we began getting more referrals from previous clients than from any other marketing source. We have established a reputation, such that if clients want to receive effective services for couples counseling, adolescent therapy, or personal growth coaching, SMC is the place to go. (Thank you, Alan).

The benefits of narrowing down your focus to three domains are:

- You increase your capabilities with all three, providing excellent client care and results.
- You are able to build a solid reputation.
- You decrease your risk of burnout, because you are working with clients who want help in the areas about which you are passionate.

I'm not saying that I never treat someone with depression or anxiety. That would be a lie. At the same time, typically when I accept a client struggling with symptoms of either depression or anxiety, the treatment frequently leads to one of my three areas of specialization. Clients end up bringing in their romantic partners or family members or needing more motivational coaching to make some changes in their lives so they could feel content again.

You truly cannot be good at everything, and the quicker you realize the benefits of narrowing your focus, the more successful you'll be as a mental health practitioner (MHP). To illustrate my point, look up almost any therapist on the *Psychology Today* directory and his or her areas of specialty and chances are you will count about 10–20 different mental health disorders that each therapist treats. In my opinion, this range includes a lot of categories, claiming the therapists' expert knowledge in each area. I'm not saying that they cannot provide effective treatment for each of the areas listed in their profiles; what I will say, however, is that I would not go to a neurologist specializing in 10–20 other fields besides neurology—would you? Because when we think about it in terms of having brain surgery, we don't want to risk having a brain surgeon that is anything less than the best, and our potential clients deserve the same expertise.

I can almost feel your anxiety rising, just thinking about narrowing down your focus to three specialty areas, but if you want to do this right, you need to consider this advice. Rather than focusing on those patients you'll not attract (because you are not marketing to the masses), you will be able to provide such exceptional care for the clientele whom you do work with that you will become highly recommended. The rave reviews of your impeccable care will nudge clients who may be out of your geographic area to travel long distances just to work with you. If this is the case, you can then expand the block of time to work with them longer than a typical 50-minute session. This is how I convince couples who want to see me but who are on the fence about committing to the commute. I tell them that greater results can be achieved if we can work with the deeper issues longer, typically speeding up the treatment process and letting them terminate it sooner than if they had a therapist closer to their home.

This field has a high burnout rate, which I believe is due to therapists trying to be too much to too many clients. They attempt to excel at everything rather than being experts in a few areas that actually excite them. The more you can stay true to what you're passionate about, the more effective you'll be with clients, the more they will come knocking on your door for your specialty care, and the more successful your practice will be.

A good idea would be to visit my website, mhprivatepractice.com, and download the business plan template. Even if you are not seeking third party financing, it is a good idea to lay out a map for your business, what you want it to stand for, how you see it growing, and milestones you hope to reach while you are a private practice owner, etc.

PART 2

# DEVELOP YOUR BRAND AND CREATE A MISSION STATEMENT

## *Develop Your Brand*

In the process of opening a business, you need to determine what the public image will be and what your practice will represent. This is part of brand development. For instance, Nike has branded themselves for athletic shoes and then expanded their brand to athletic apparel. When you create a brand you are building an association for the public to remember the practice. For example, lets say you specialize in couples grief and if you have done your job in branding that service with your practice. When someone either loses a partner or a friend becomes a widow, they will think of your practice when considering grief counseling. Through brand associations, you have linked a service to your practice. That is why it is important to stick close to your three areas of expertise in order to build a rememberable brand. Next, we will construct a mission statement, which will help guide business decisions and keep you faithful to your public image.

### *Mission Statement*

At this time, you will formulate the mission statement for your private practice. For example, SMC's primary goal is to offer effective therapeutic services by highly trained MHPs. We market to populations from higher socioeconomic levels. Ours is a fee-for-service practice that provides a secure and tasteful space for clients to come and share their stories. Additionally, as anonymity is very important to our clients, it's also important to us; we'll work to the best of our ability to ensure maximum confidentiality.

A mission statement would be similar to the bumper pads we used at the bowling alley when we were kids. Combined with a strong idea of what your brand will represent, your mission statement will keep you on the right path and out of the gutter. In this case a gutter is a population that you have no interest in treating. There might be a slow period in business, during which you may be tempted to jump on opportunities that are technically within the "gutter"; a mission statement, however, will prevent you from mistakenly straying into that gutter and losing focus of your primary goals. Consider, for example the following scenario:

Maybe your passion is to provide services to underprivileged children, and you don't ever want to lose sight of what this type of work means to you. Here is an example of a mission statement. "Our mission is to provide mental health services to underserved populations. To ensure that our clients have the type of mental health services they deserve and maintain the right to receive them, we'll provide office locations that are easy to access with convenient public transportation." Note that this mission statement will help guide you when you are looking for office spaces or if you are offered an opportunity to expand in a suitable neighborhood. However, if the office location is far from any public transportation hub, you will have to either reconsider your mission statement or decline the opportunity.

If you need some ideas to help spark your creative writing side, simply do a Google search of other mission statements and read until you become inspired. I have also provided a free mission statement development template on my website, mhprivatepractice.com. Remember that a mission statement is intended to help guide you through decision making, expanding, and restructuring. Think long and hard about your mission statement, so when the time comes, it will serve you well.

When you're ready, let's move along to the next stage—determining the right location for your private practice, in which it's important to consider the *market saturation and the market's need for your services.*

# PART 3

# MARKET SATURATION AND DEMAND FOR SERVICES

## *Market Saturation*

You are cruising right along and putting together a solid plan for your private practice. In this section, we will dream a bit, and then vet it with some fact-checking. Consider three possible geographic locations for your private practice:

1. First choice – Perfect! This is the most desirable place.
2. Second choice – Great spot! It's just not my ideal fantasy.
3. Third choice – Good. Definitely doable.

Once you have three potential locations selected, you need to do some research to determine if the market (your select population) is saturated with other MHPs. To begin, simply perform a Google search.

Type in "find a therapist in [name of city]" and "find a counselor in [name of city]." Next, repeat the same search, but add in your three specialty areas. For example, "Find a grief counselor in [name of city]." Then browse the top therapist directories in your area, such as *Psychology Today*, and search your three locations to see how many MHPs are practicing in those cities.

*What Did You Find?*

Based on your results, you may need to perform a closer examination of the potential sites. If you searched, and your number one choice is not saturated, then great! You can move on to the next section—determining if there is a demand for services. Whatever you do, don't assume it's a good location because few therapists have tapped in; be curious and make sure that there are no detrimental reasons why other MHPs have not entered into the area.

Returning to your probable search results, you may have found that your third option is the least saturated; however, it is your least favorite site.

At this time, let us re-evaluate the three locations. Consider:

- Which is closest to your home or has a minimally stressful commute?
- Which is located in a trendy (underserved, underprivileged, or whatever is your target population) neighborhood?
- Which is located near a business complex?
- Which has elements of nature and a calm landscape surrounding it?
- Which is in a city that has a good reputation for supporting local businesses?

- Which has the population you wish to serve?
- Which has your target socioeconomic population?
- Which has a high population density?

Now based on your reasons for each location, make a pros-and-cons list for each. For example: Table 1 below provides an example of a pros-and-cons list comparing the three locations.

**TABLE 1**

*Compares the pros-and-cons of the three potential office locations.*

| Location # | Pros | Cons |
| --- | --- | --- |
| 1 | Trendy | Saturated |
| | By a business park | Longer commute |
| 2 | High socioeconomic class | High lease rates |
| | Good reputation for supporting small businesses | Saturated |
| | High population density | Business park only |
| 3 | Close to home | Not as trendy |
| | Low saturation | Residential, retail, and business park |

We can see that although location number three was last on our list, because the market is not saturated here, it actually presents a good opportunity to conduct more research.

### *Demand for Services*

To determine if there is a need for your services in the location you choose to explore further, you need to leave the computer and go out to the field. You will need to do the following:

- Consult the Chamber of Commerce representatives.
- Sit in on a local Rotary lunch meeting and talk to some of the community members.
- Visit the schools and ask the school officials what needs are not being met at this time.
- Visit local churches and ask the pastors and volunteers what they notice as the greatest needs, in terms of mental health services.
- Chat with hairdressers. They resemble us in that they listen to their clients' troubles and have an insider's perspective on what the community needs.
- Display a survey box at a few locations, such as a 24-hour fitness facility, 24-hour grocery store, or anywhere else that you think would help you obtain the appropriate information.

After you have selected a spot that has low to medium saturation as well as demand for your services, we can proceed with some number crunching! Two major steps that are commonly missed when starting a business are figuring out what sort of lifestyle you want as a business owner and determining how much overhead you want to manage. In other words, you need to determine how much time you want to work (how tied to the business you want to be), and how much money you want to owe each month to manage your practice. In Step Two: Ideal Lifestyle and Realistic Budget Planning, we're going to explore theses considerations and more. By the end of the next section, you'll have a budget in mind, clarity about what type of lifestyle you desire, and a greater understanding of why it's imperative to take this step now before you consider potential office locations.

STEP TWO

# IDEAL LIFESTYLE AND REALISTIC BUDGET PLANNING

# PART I

# WHAT IS YOUR IDEAL LIFESTYLE?

Lifestyle concerns may seem off-topic; however, it's actually one of the most important questions you need to ask yourself before going any further. I recommend that you clearly lay out how you want your practice to help facilitate the lifestyle you desire. Too often, people can initiate a business deal without considering the time it will take to earn the money they envision or how much stress it will add to their lives. I ask you again: what kind of lifestyle do you want to have while you are a private practice owner?

- How many days per week do you want to work? If you prefer to work 2–3 days (like myself), then keep this in mind when planning the budget. If you're not careful, you can wind up having to double the days worked per week just to pay the bills.
- What sort of hours do you plan on working? Let's say you have a family with young children for whom you want to be home each night to tuck them into bed. You need to plan ahead and think about the clientele you wish to serve. If you are planning on treating adolescents, remember that

during the school year, your day won't officially begin until after 3 p.m. Now factor in that your preference to work for only 2–3 days would give you very limited time to see clients and arrive home to tuck your kids in.

- Do you like to take vacations? If you are like me and enjoy a good mini-vacation here and there, you will want to have the freedom to jet off when you find opportunities to do so. Going too far over your head financially may hinder you from taking that week off from seeing clients.

- Are you an MHP who practices good self-care? For example, I know that when I'm getting too tired with work, I need to be able to ease back on my caseload. If this is the case for you, you'll want to make sure you have the freedom to slow down your role a bit at the practice and take care of yourself.

- What are the five things you value most in life? If you value family time or showing up at your child's extracurricular events, you should plan ahead in order to manage your work schedule and finances so that you can be where you desire when you want to be there. Let's say your yoga class is what gives you fuel for the week, and you get so invested financially that when things slow down, you decide to fill the slot with a client rather than keeping it blocked off for your sacred me-time. What do you think is going to happen then?

These are only a few examples of things you need to consider seriously before starting the process of owning your business. Being a business owner is seductive and comes with the risk of sucking you in. Without a clear understanding of your desired lifestyle, you have the potential of creating a nightmare rather than a practice that supports your dreams.

The following is how I determined the sort of lifestyle I wanted:

I knew before I opened SMC that I would only work 2–3 days, because my roles as a wife and mother are my priorities. Therefore, in all my pre-calculations (a task you will perform next), I factored in how often I would allow myself to be pulled away from my family. I also wasn't going to give up on my hobbies for the sake of making money. I frequently book trips and overnight getaways for my husband and me, so I had to make sure I would not get so strapped for cash that I would be tied to the office on weekends.

As you can see, determining your preferred lifestyle before developing a practice is a crucial step that needs to be carefully considered. Later in this section, I will introduce you to an MHP named Brenda. She didn't think this part through too well and ended up seriously regretting the fact.

I have created a free template available for download on my website, mhprivatepractice.com, which will help you hone in on what is most important to you in terms of values and how you'd like your business to support the lifestyle you desire.

PART II

# HOW MUCH OVERHEAD IS TOO MUCH?

Now that you have been very thoughtful in clarifying your preferred lifestyle as a practice owner, you need to come up with an amount that will enable your desired lifestyle rather than limit or take away what you value most. Before you go out and look at potential lease spaces, you should crunch the numbers. The dollar amount that must be determined is based on:

## *How Much Overhead Do You Want?*

This is an essential question in business that many skip over. Let's compare two MHPs who opened up their own private practices. The difference between the two was that one crunched the numbers and determined what kind of lifestyle she wanted her business to facilitate, and the other did not.

### *Brenda's Blunder*

Brenda wanted to open a private practice in an upscale, trendy neighborhood just off the bay. The potential office location was quite a drive from her residence, but she didn't think the commute would be too bad. She envisioned sitting in the local coffee shop, sipping on an overpriced cup of joe as she prepared for cases. The day she went to look at some spaces, there was one particular office that she knew—the moment she walked in—had to be hers! It was trimmed with thick, dark wood panels and had exposed brick in the main office interior, a large conference room that she would never use, and four, extra-large pane windows facing the water. People always told her to trust her gut, yet even though she was a little concerned about starting a new practice in a community to which she did not yet belong and about leasing a space this expensive, she hit the override button and pushed past the misgivings created by her sixth sense. She looked at one more space a block up from the water, (and sneered her nose at it), and signed a three-year lease that day for the first space. *Some things are simply meant to be*, she told herself.

While furnishing her new office, Brenda was amazed at all the financing promotions available. She decided to go all out and provide a rich environment for her clients. She financed the furniture, office equipment, wall décor, window treatments, and even a beverage center. The ease in which everything all came together really surprised her. The fact that she hadn't hit any bumps thus far only reassured her that she had made the right decision in leasing the new office.

Then a few months went by, and she only managed to reel in a handful of clients. She began nervously sorting through the incessant bills that kept rolling in, creating piles of "pay now," "hold on paying," and "call for an extension." Then she did what a lot of new business owners do in this boat . . . she panicked.

*Sandra's Success*

Meanwhile, in the same part of town, Sandra was starting her own journey of becoming a private practice owner. She had been saving her money for quite some time and knew exactly how much she was willing to spend on an office, because she did not want all the overhead of occupying a space that exceeded her price range. Her lifestyle was similar to a surfer, if you will. She enjoyed her job immensely but loved living life even more. She wanted to find a place within her budget for her to work enough to pay the bills and make a decent income.

Coincidentally, she leased the same space that Brenda had sneered at condescendingly. A smaller office about a block away from the main street, it was simple but well kept. It had one large window to let in natural light, was priced below her budget, and was perfect!

Weeks before Sandra began this process, she crunched the numbers to determine what she could make work. She knew how much she could spend on her monthly lease, utilities, furnishings, and miscellaneous costs; when she came up with these numbers, she factored in the slow times as well. She did choose to finance most of her furnishings but did so knowing that she already had enough savings to pay everything off if she wanted.

During those first few months, Sandra saw the same number of clients that Brenda did, and when the bills came in, she simply wrote the checks. She was very comfortable in her decision to open a private practice and was excited to see what was to come. One of her biggest fears in opening her own business was that she would become married to it and be unable to maintain her lifestyle, but because she had thought everything through, she was able to have both—a business and a great life outside of work.

As you can see, knowing your finances is a crucial step in this process, and as Sandra illustrated, knowing what you want in terms of your lifestyle is also key.

**TABLE 2**

*Comparison of the Total Overhead between Brenda and Sandra*

| **Monthly Bills** | **Brenda** | **Sandra** |
|---|---|---|
| Lease | $2,200 | $600 |
| Internet/phone | $200 | $130<br>(uses Google # for phone) |
| Heating/cooling | $100 | Included |
| Garbage | $20 | Included |
| Electronic health records | $150 | $60 |
| Furniture | $400 | $60 |
| Computer/printer | $50 | $15 |
| Décor | $80 | $20 |
| Office supplies | $25 | $25 |
| Subscriptions | $80 | $80 |
| Association dues/insurance | $410 | $410 |
| **Total** | **$3,715** | **$1,400** |

Now to determine how many hours each MHP would have to work before reaching the breakeven point, let's set a generic rate at $100 per session and assume that they both want to work 20 hours per week.

**TABLE 3**

*Hours Needed to Work Per Month to Pay Cost per Month (CPM) and Total Gross Income (TGI)*

| MHP | CPM/$100 | #Hours/ Month | #Hours Remaining/ Month | TGI/ Month | TGI/ Year 1 |
|---|---|---|---|---|---|
| Brenda | $3,715/100 = 37.15 | 38 | 80-38=42 | $100x42= $4,200 | $4,200x12= $50,400 |
| Sandra | $1,400/100 =14 | 14 | 80-14=66 | $100x66= $6,600 | $6,600x12= $79,200 |

Let me explain how I obtained these numbers. By dividing the total CPM amount by the rate of a typical session (you could plug in your hourly rate to get a more accurate prediction), I obtained the number of sessions each month needed to pay for the expenses. Then I deducted the number of sessions per month needed to cover costs from the total number of sessions worked (80/month), and then multiplied that by the session rate ($100) to get the monthly TGI, followed by the annual TGI. As you can see, Brenda is at quite a disadvantage. Let's take this one step further and compare the difference in earnings over the course of their lease term, which is huge!

**TABLE 4**

*Annual Difference in Income between the Two MHPs*

| Year 1 Difference | Year 2 Difference | Year 3 Difference |
|---|---|---|
| $28,800 | $57,600 | $86,400 |

These are fictitious numbers, of course; however, they're reasonably accurate, based on typical expenses in Minnesota. You can see why it's important to take the time to punch in the calculations prior to visiting any potential spaces. This is where a business venture can totally go beyond our grasp. We tend to favor an attractive space (that often times comes at a high cost to lease) and justify why we deserve a nice location and how it will serve our needs better. However, knowing your budget will help you stay focused so that you will only look at spaces within your price range and not be tempted to go over it.

If Brenda wants to make as much money as Sandra, she will have to sacrifice her time and work more hours, which she failed to consider when she made her decisions. Is she stuck in this mess for the full three years? No, Brenda can certainly take several actions to decrease her financial burden:

- Hire an Independent Contractor (IC)
- Bring on a partner or partners to share the debt and shift to a group practice
- Sublet to other MHPs and share the space

I don't want you to feel like I am trying to frighten you. My intention is to give you a clear example of what can be a catastrophic error in the business world if you do not determine your budget and do not consider the lifestyle you want as a private practice owner. In order to help determine your CPM, I have included a budget template on my website, mhprivatepractice.com; simply download the free form and complete.

At this stage, we'll proceed in the direction of helping you move into your new space. Next, I'll go over some simple tips and tricks that will help you find the perfect spot to open a private practice, negotiate the lease terms, and decrease your financial risk.

### *Finding the Right Space*

Here are a few details that may be overlooked in the excitement of the moment while searching for potential spaces.

- Make sure you find a space that is in a safe area, well lit at night, and not too isolated for you, your clients, and your contractors to be walking out in the dark.
- This may seem like overkill, but I suggest visiting a space that you really like multiple times at various periods throughout the day. This will give you a true experience of what the noise level will be (very important in our field).
- Inspect the heating and cooling features. Ensure that the office is well ventilated and, if possible, that you have your own thermostat. Seeing clients back-to-back creates a stuffy office in a hurry.

- If you have gone through the pros-and-cons process and, on paper, know that a space should be "right," yet have a foreboding to walk away, trust your gut instincts-and walk away. I believe that we have a sixth sense communicating to us, one that can foresee problems or dangers. You cannot cover up a bad feeling with a coat of paint. If you feel uncomfortable in the space, chances are your clients will experience the same feeling. You want to steer away from that threat as much as possible. Choose a space that is inviting and that creates an atmosphere where clients will frequently tell you *I don't want to leave* or *I wish my home felt this great.*

- Negotiating the lease terms is completely normal and should be expected. Some questions that you can ask include:

    - If I sign a longer lease period, can I decrease my monthly overhead (lease payment)?

    - Would you consider a longer-term lease with an option for me to give 90 days' notice to terminate the agreement if I add value to the space? An example would be adding a lobby area or something else that enhances the value of the space and that you cannot take with you when you leave.

    - What signage am I allowed to have, and how soon can I install it?

- Make certain that you ask about utilities and what is included in the lease price. If it's not all-inclusive, inquire about the average CPM. Ask about the Internet; if you need to supply that, check with other tenants for accuracy about the given CPM and suggest the option of sharing the Internet service.

- Talk to other tenants about how responsive the landlord/ owner is when you need something or when something is broken. For example, if you work in an area where it snows, you want to make sure you have a landlord that beats everyone to the office and shovels the sidewalks. Additionally, ask them about the noise level; if at times it does get noisier, find out if this occurs during your counseling hours, and so on. Check to see what hours the other tenants occupy the building. It's very important for personal security to try your best to find a building where you're not alone in your practice, especially because of the work we do and the time of night that we typically see clients.

- Read the lease very carefully. Determine if there are any rules around painting and nail holes. A colleague once told me she had to pay $50/nail hole because she only skimmed the lease terms and conditions and then went overboard with the wall décor.

# PART III

# MANAGE RISKS

When you are just starting out, it is a good idea to consider possible options for decreasing the financial risk. You may live in a part of the world where lease rates are sky high, so finding a partner (or partners) will be beneficial or necessary. Other options would be to (1) start smaller and work your way into a bigger space once you have established your practice within the desired community, (2) sign a shorter-termed lease by increasing your costs per month, (3) sublet the space to other MHPs, or (4) if you can cover the costs per month, you may decide to bring on ICs. Below is a list of tables that evaluate some pros and cons to each risk-reducing method.

**TABLE 5**

*Pros and Cons of Starting a Group Practice*

| Pros | Cons |
|---|---|
| A shared office space decreases time you spend alone in the office. | You're not exclusively in charge of day-to-day operations; every decision would be a group decision. |
| You could afford a better space if more people shared the financial burden. | |
| You have the ability to consult with colleagues more frequently and are not providing therapy solely on your own. | |

**TABLE 6**

*Pros and Cons of Starting with a Smaller Space until Reputation Is Built*

| Pros | Cons |
|---|---|
| There is not as much overhead. | You would have to do the makeover and the entire process again when you move into a larger space. |
| You don't have to bring on other partners and share power. | |

**TABLE 7**

*Pros and Cons of Decreasing Length of Lease and Paying More Each Month*

| Pros | Cons |
|---|---|
| You are not as scared to commit to a lease for your practice, since you know the agreed duration is cut in half. | You're starting a baby company with more overhead each month. |

**TABLE 8**

*Pros and Cons of Subletting the Space to Other MHPs*

| Pros | Cons |
|---|---|
| You can share the Cost Per Month. | Sharing office space can become tricky or may limit opportunities to see clients. |
| | It can become annoying having to change therapy supplies each time you come in. |
| | You don't make passive income from MHPs like you would if they were ICs. |
| | You have multiple entities practicing out of the same space. |

**TABLE 9**

*Pros and Cons of Hiring an IC*

| Pros | Cons |
|---|---|
| Make passive income. | There may be scheduling conflicts. |
| Create a greater awareness of your practice in the community by gaining the ability to serve more clients. | You have limited control on how they do therapy, since they are not W-2 employees. |
| Decrease your financial burden. | |
| You don't have to perform a lot of managerial tasks as you would if they were W-2 employees. | |

I believe that if you have the investment money and are able to start paying the total CPM on your own, the best route is to bring on ICs right away. In the next section, I will give more details about why I believe this is a good business decision.

### *Adding Independent Contractors Right Away Is a Smart Move*

One of my colleagues waited until he had a full caseload before bringing anyone on because he wanted to work over 40 client hours a week. By contrast, I knew that I wanted minimum work hours. I like to work just enough to pay the bills and save some money; after that, I enjoy my lifestyle of being a wife and a mom to our young kids. For these reasons, bringing on ICs was a no-brainer for me. The nice office I had created sat idle most of the week. As a business person, it made sense to bring on ICs right away, start increasing our impact on the community (drawing more attention to our practice), and make money to put toward the CPM.

Let me illustrate how you go about bringing on ICs. First, decide how many hours you want to work per week and determine if you want to see your clients back-to-back for 7–10 hours straight or break up the timetable into 4–6-hour blocks. As you are formulating your ideal work week, make sure you factor in your population and when they can be seen; for example, teens would need to be seen after 3 o' clock in the afternoon most days. This is my ideal schedule for 16–20 client hours per week:

Monday: 8:00 a.m. – 12:00 p.m.

Wednesday: 8:00 a.m. – 7:00 p.m.

Thursday: 8:00 a.m. – 8:00 p.m.

<u>That leaves plenty of hours for one or more ICs:</u>

Monday: 1:00 p.m. – 8:00 p.m.

Tuesday: 8:00 a.m. – 8:00 p.m.

Friday: 8:00 a.m. – 5:00 p.m.

Saturday:8:00 a.m. – 5:00 p.m.

The above schedule totals 40 hours to split between or among 2–3 ICs! Hire them and start each with a 4-hour block of time, and then expand from there. For example, my ICs started with:

First IC:Monday: 5:00 p.m. – 9:00 p.m.

Second IC:Tuesday:4:00 p.m. – 8:00 p.m.

Third IC:Saturday: 12:00 p.m. – 4:00 p.m.

*What Is a Standard Compensation Split?*

In this industry, it is common to start with an IC at a 60/40 split; they take home 60% of their earnings, and you keep 40%. At SMC, I have chosen to start the split at 70/30; once the IC maintains more than eight clients per week, the ratio changes to 75/25. I do so for several reasons, but the main one is for company morale. I intend to train people and have them stay over the long term. I don't want them feeling undervalued or unappreciated when they work for me. I want them to know that if they were to leave, there is little chance they would be able to earn better income, work in a nicer space, or feel more a part of a group-like practice, without having any skin in the game. My ICs mean the world to me; they represent the SMC brand, and it is my job to always make them feel that I acknowledge all they do for the company.

In order to illustrate the passive income that can be made from bringing on ICs, let's consider the following scenario. If your three ICs average seven client hours per week, and their average session rate is $100, you would make roughly $630 per week, $2520 per month, and $30,240 per year or $90,720 over the course of the three-year lease. If we take it one step further and add that into Sandra's total, she would be bringing in on average per year $109,440 (and $328,320 for the full lease term of three years). Now imagine if she were able to generate a few streams of passive income along with this salary: I am positive she would be more than doubling her paycheck or even tripling her paycheck as an owner versus an IC working for another practice. Remember that these are conservative numbers and most certainly can be achieved.

> The formula to calculate the possible income from your ICs is:
>
> (Total number of client hours from your ICs) x (Session rate) x (Percentage that the practice keeps) = (Income per week from ICs) x (4 weeks in a month) = (Income per month from ICs) x (12 months in a year) = (Income per year from ICs) x (Length of lease term in years) = (Total income from ICs over the course of the lease term).

If I can offer you one piece of advice about bringing on ICs, it would be to treat them well. Leave them notes about how much you appreciate them, or present an accolade for something you know they did really well. Give them gifts for the holidays and occasional bonuses, spend some time making their birthdays special, and so on. Give them your time when they ask for it. When my contractors are nervous, especially at the start of their practice, it is much like holding a toddler's hand when walking into a busy room. They may be timid, but if they know that the owner of the private practice is a simple text away to calm their nerves in the beginning weeks, it means a lot to them. You're helping them become the very best they can be, hence accomplishing great work and building a reputation that lines up with your mission statement and brand. It is a win-win situation for everyone.

*TIP*

*When hiring ICs, try and only hire on a referral basis. You will have colleagues that will recommend contractors that would be a good fit for your brand, and I highly suggest that you go with referrals rather than posting a job opening ad. I have done both, and luckily, two have been fabulous; however, I did have one that came from a job posting that could have potentially turned into a nightmare if I had not been careful in letting her go. I would rather you dodge that bullet than have to learn from the same mistake. Take the safe route and only bring on referred ICs!*

# STEP THREE

# BUILDING A SOLID INFRASTRUCTURE

# PART I

# MAKING YOUR PRACTICE LEGITIMATE

## *Practice Name*

Now that you have created your brand, found a community in need of your services, and crunched the numbers, it's time to build some infrastructure.

The first task on your agenda is to pick out a name for your private practice. When you start to brainstorm, don't go straight to all the warm and fuzzy descriptive words, such as "Pathways to Happiness." This is a great tagline; however, you want your name to contain keywords that your target market will search for. For example, SMC is located in the south metro portion of Minnesota. I combined two keywords commonly searched together: "south metro" and "counseling." I put a lot of thought into the name because I wanted to increase my company's chances of appearing on the first page of a Google search. Another detail to pay attention to is the name's length: when a prospective client is typing in a domain web address, the longer and trickier it is (with an underscore, etc.), the greater the chances of the client making typographical errors—and never landing on your website. Keep its name short, and use keywords.

### *Domain Name*

Next, log on to GoDaddy (or any other domain purchasing site) and type in your private practice name to see if it's taken. If this is the case, you have some options: you can play with the name, or simply add your state or province initials at the end. For example, if southmetrocounseling.com had been taken, I could have changed it to southmetrocounselingmn.com.

### *Business Structure*

After you purchase your domain name, you are ready to structure your business. There are several types of business structures to choose from; however, the most common for a private practice would be a sole proprietorship or limited liability company. You can visit any website that offers services in structuring business, or perform a web search, such as "how to structure my business in [enter your state or province]." You are creating a business structure to protect your personal assets should your company ever get sued and for easier tax preparation.

For example, if you live in the state of Minnesota:

1. Go to sos.state.mn.us.
2. Click on "Forms and Publications."
3. Click on "Business and Non-Profit Forms."
4. Read more about which type of corporation you would like your practice to be. The most common is LLC, followed by S-Corp.
5. After selecting the type under which you would like to file your private practice, follow the prompts.

Now I can't do this for each state or province, but this will give you a template to follow, whichever part of the world you have your practice.

### *Sales Tax ID and Federal Employee Identification Number*

In order to obtain a sales tax ID, you'll need to go through a similar process as you did above in developing a business structure. The method will vary between state and province; therefore, I suggest Googling "how to obtain a sales tax ID in [name of city]." For example, in Minnesota you will need to first attain a federal employee identification number or (FEIN), and then you can proceed to get your sales tax ID. Please see the reference list at the end of the book for a website link to the IRS and a phone number to call for a FEIN. The following is a list of information that you will need to have ready in order to obtain your FEIN:

- Business name
- Address of the practice
- What type of business structure it is (for example, sole proprietorship or limited liability company)
- Name of the owner(s)
- Estimated number of employees

### *Logo Design*

Since most of us are not graphic designers, I suggest hiring a professional to design your logo. Similar to what I did, you can visit Elance.com, or other established and reputable freelance job boards, sign up, and post an advertisement looking for a graphic designer to create a simple logo. A slew of designers will then submit bids to you, stating how long it will take and how much they will charge per hour. The logo for SMC only took four days to complete, and I spent $56 (+$30 tip) for it. You'll want a logo for the next project, which is paperwork!

## PART II

# CREATING DOCUMENTS AND FORMS

This should be an exciting section because you are making your private practice more legitimate and official. Here are some of the forms you will want to have ready prior to opening your practice:

- Notice of Privacy Practices
- Client Bill of Rights
- Permission to Consult
- Release of Information
- Informed Consent
- Authorization to Process Credit Card Payments
- Intake Packets
    - Couples
    - Families

    - Children/Adolescents
    - Individuals
- IC Contract

You can find online examples for each form by simply Googling the form title. You will notice that many include similar content, and the main detail that changes is the name of the private practice. Alternatively, you can download a template from my website, mhprivatepractice.com and simply make the changes needed to create a document that meets the needs of your practice, taking care to add your logo.

### *Changing Your Insurance Policy*

Don't forget to contact your insurance provider and change the type of coverage you have from IC to private practice owner. The premium should only increase by approximately $30 per year, so do not worry about this change. I have two million-dollar policies; one is necessary, and the second is just in case.

### *Business Cards and Marketing Materials*

We are getting closer! It's time to order your business cards with your fancy logo, as well as other marketing materials. When you are thinking about designing your materials, do so in terms of the customers you intend to attract. For SMC, we want to appeal to populations from the high socioeconomic bracket, so our materials are elegant and simple. Stay true to your brand, and think about what message you want to convey based on the materials.

Personally, I am a frequent user of Vistaprint and have been very satisfied with their products. I know there are many other reputable print companies that produce quality products; simply find one that best suits your needs.

In terms of other marketing materials, such as flyers, I suggest hiring a graphic designer to ensure a professional, polished look. For MHPs who lack an artistic touch, the do-it-yourself option is not advisable (just like with your logo design). Moreover, a professional graphic artist makes sure that the message, branding, style, colors, etc. are consistent across all marking materials (as well as with the website).

For other marketing ideas, please jump ahead to Step Four: Spreading the News.

### *Scheduling Made Simple*

If you follow my advice and bring on ICs, create a scheduling system that everyone can see no matter where they are. You have several options; here are a few that I have found helpful:

- Google Calendar
- The calendar on your email platform (such as GoDaddy)
- The calendar on your electronic health records (EHRs) platform

We have chosen to use Google Calendar due to its accessibility on our mobile and personal electronic devices.

### *How to Set up a Google Calendar for Your Business*

1. Whether or not you have a personal Gmail account, you will want to create an email account just for the practice. For example, I created southmetrocounseling@gmail.com. Have each IC create a Gmail account if he or she does not have one yet.

2. Go to your calendar. On the left-hand margin, you will see "Other Calendars" and a box where you can *"add a friend's calendar."* Simply add one IC email address at a time and click "invite." The ICs will need to do the same with your email address and those of the other ICs. Everyone invites everyone else; this is how you get a shared business calendar.

3. I suggest advising your ICs to type "OPEN" in the hour blocks when you are free to schedule them with potential clients. The last thing you want to do when you have a client on the line ready to be reeled in is have to postpone booking the client and get back to them later because you must first check to determine when an IC will be available. Book clients ASAP by having ICs mark their availability each week.

## PART III

# BUILDING A WEBSITE

You're at the point in this journey to start constructing your website. Before you balk, thinking *that is not my strong point,* I suggest visiting squarespace.com or other well-crafted web designing platforms that allow you to make your website unique while maintaining professionalism, and look over some sample templates. Now this is a laborious task; however, I really encourage you to steer away from the cookie-cutter therapy sites with the soft greens and rocks on the home screen. I believe that if you intend to set yourself apart from other practitioners, the best thing you can do for your practice is to invest time in creating a unique site that is not a replica of hundreds of other MHP sites.

For the MHPs who may be clueless about website design or have no time or inclination for it, I suggest an alternative (other than a cookie cutter site), such as commissioning a web designer to develop the website and upgrade, update, or maintain the site on an as-needed basis. You will still need to work closely with the web developer in all stages of the design process to ensure that the company's mission, brand, objectives, etc. are conveyed clearly and consistently. Communicate with the web developer the specific needs and preferences of the target market, etc.

For illustrative purposes, let's say you went to Squarespace and found a template that you'd like to play with. You can sign up for a free, two-week trial and actually begin setting up your site with photos, blog posts, and other content. Before the trial ends, make sure you upgrade your account; otherwise, you will lose all the content that you worked on the previous 13 days. Whatever you do, don't skimp on this process! You literally have a few seconds to grab your potential clients' attention and draw them into your site; if it is a cheap, halfway-put-together site, they will bounce, and your competitor will thank you.

### *A Guide to Completing Your Website*

1. Surf the Internet until you find a website that truly catches your attention. Choose a design that looks professional and appealing to your target market (always remember that you are not the customer, so go for what *your clientele* would like), and that represents your brand well.

2. Visit Squarespace.com, or other website design platforms, and set up a two-week free trial. Search through the various templates and see which one pulls you in the most (again keeping in mind your target market; for example, if you are working with patients suffering from trauma, don't choose one with flashy pop-ups, etc.).

3. Go to a respectable website that sells photos, such as istock.com (or shutterstock.com, gettyimages.com, or 123rf.com), set up an account, and add the selected photos (with white backgrounds) to your cart. Save the pictures

but don't purchase them all right away, because you want to make sure your selections mesh well with your website layout. This is like picking out samples of paint colors and other products like flooring and trim—you want to bring them home to see if they all match perfectly.

4. Pull the trigger. With your basic layout completed, you are ready to import the photos and adjust the content. Your next step is to simply upgrade and sign up with whichever web design company and photo retailer you have chosen.

Should you decide to do it yourself, your website will take you the longest to complete out of all the tasks in this book. That's okay; it's necessary to truly put your heart and soul into the website. Most web design platforms, such as Squarespace, Wix, or Weebly, offer excellent search engine optimization (SEO) services that are standard when you sign up, so that part is taken care of, and you don't have to worry about hiring a professional to do that task. Make your content count by including keywords in the page titles and the photo descriptions, etc. There are several free videos that provide useful information regarding the process, either on your web design platform or on YouTube.

If you are unaware of the keywords that your target audience is searching, go to spyfu.com and begin by researching what your competitors use as keywords in their advertising.

## PART IV

# CHOOSING AN ELECTRONIC HEALTH RECORDS (EHRS) PLATFORM

Depending on which state or province you have your practice, the EHRs mandate may not have been issued yet. Here in Minnesota, as of 2015, we are required to have all client files on an approved EHRs platform. There are several to choose from; if you simply perform a Google search of a comparison review of the top 10 EHRs platforms that are HIPPA compliant, you will be able to find one that will meet the needs of your practice.

In our case, SMC ended up choosing a simple EHRs platform: it is reasonably priced, simple to learn, and has exactly what we need for the size of our practice. For me, this is money well spent, because its little "to-do" reminders each time I log in help me stay on top of treatment plans, case notes, primary care physician releases, and other necessary paperwork.

# PART V

# OPTING FOR FEE-FOR-SERVICE OR INSURANCE-BASED PRACTICE

I was able to start my own pre-licensure, private practice by having a fee-for-service practice. Fee-for-service means that the clients pay out of pocket, and insurance is not accepted to pay for services. Some MHPs may ask how it is possible to make a living from a fee-for-service practice, especially after the Obama Care Act (in the U.S.). Well, it is possible: I have been making a decent income now for three years, and knock on wood, my income keeps increasing as the years go on (as it should). Let's look at some options, so you can choose how you want to proceed.

## *Non-Licensed Practitioner Hiring a Licensed Consultant Option*

If you are in the same boat as I am and are not a licensed professional, you can still open a practice that accepts insurance; you just have to hire a licensed professional as a consultant for your practice. It means that he or she would come to your practice for a set number of hours each week to review and approve of any diagnostic assessments that need to be submitted to the insurance companies for reimbursement. If you choose this route, make sure you calculate the costs and benefits of doing so, because you will be paying a portion of your earnings to the consultant. If the numbers are in your favor, this may be a good choice to explore. Before you do anything, I suggest calling all insurance panels on which you would like to get your practice credentialed and inquiring if they would approve a licensed consultant. If so, ask about the required credentials for the licensed consultant, such as licensed psychologist, licensed marriage and family therapist, or licensed professional counselor.

### *Licensed Professional Option*

If you are a licensed professional and opt for an insurance-based practice, you simply have to contact each one of the insurance panels on which you wish to be credentialed, go through the application process, and wait. You can still start a fee-for-service practice until you obtain approval.

### *Fee-for-Service Option*

As I have explained, SMC is a straight fee-for-service practice. I have been surprised by some colleagues' reactions when they find out this fact. The majority of responses are skeptical and fear based.

*I just don't see how that could generate income.*

*I could never do fee for service; I would starve.*

*I have always wanted to try fee for service*
*but just never had the guts.*

Granted, most practitioners have a broader population of patients. I have very specific populations whom I treat, most of whom are happy to pay out of pocket. Couples counseling is still not a priority for insurance companies; if they happen to cover some family sessions, oftentimes it is very limited in terms of the treatment length and services they deem necessary. For teens, parents want to try to protect their child as much as possible; once we explain that if insurance is used, their child must be diagnosed with a mental health disorder that will go on his or her permanent medical record in order to receive treatment, they will likely understand why we have chosen to run a fee-for-service practice. Moreover, in my third specialty, personal growth, nobody wants to be diagnosed with an mental health disorder just to receive some motivational coaching. Thus, I understand that my specialty areas influence how well my practice thrives on a fee-for-service basis, and this should be considered when you are choosing which way you want to go.

### *Fee-for-Service and Insurance-Based Option*

You can do both, offer fee-for-service and get on some insurance panels. Understand, however that if you are on a specific insurance panel that reimburses less than you would make if your practice was straight fee-for-service, and a client comes in and wants to use that insurance provider, you must accept him or her; you cannot decline the use of that insurance. For example, in Minnesota there is a state assistance program (MA), which typically reimburses lower than other insurance providers. Let's say you receive a referral who wants to use MA; regardless of how you feel about MA, its low pay, the length of time it takes to be reimbursed, and so on, you must allow the client to use it since you're an approved provider for MA. Be strategic when deciding which insurance panels to apply for. Begin with the ones that pay the best and fastest, and then work your way down to the lesser-paying providers and those that are slower to reimburse.

## TABLE 10

*Pros and Cons of Having a Fee-for-Service versus Insurance-Based Practice*

| Fee for Service | | Insurance Based | |
|---|---|---|---|
| **Pros** | **Cons** | **Pros** | **Cons** |
| You are paid more quickly. | You need to create your own stream of clients. | Your practice is put on a provider's list, which refers clients to you. | There is a longer reimbursement time. |
| Treatment is not dictated by an insurance provider. | Not everyone can afford to pay out of pocket. | Most clients have insurance, and so you are likely to grow your case load more quickly. | Treatment is dictated by an insurance provider. |
| You see more clients because you spend less time on paperwork. | There can be slow periods; for example, around specific holidays or travel seasons. Families spend money on other things. | You have a steady stream of clients year round. | You see fewer clients because you spend more time on paperwork. |
| You set your rates. | You have to manage the money, credit card processing, checks, and cash. | Your reimbursement is deposited directly to your checking account. | Insurance providers set your rates. |

### *Fee-for-Service Process*

Since this process is typically the most daunting for potential, private practice owners, I will walk you through this in a step-by-step fashion. For a fee-for-service practice, find a reputable credit card processing center, such as PayPal, to enable your business to accept all major credit cards and health savings accounts (HSAs). You will also accept checks and cash as payment methods. How you collect money for each session is up to you, but I find that the most successful method is to either have the client prepay before the session or pay at the start rather than at the end. If you are fortunate enough to have a receptionist collect and process payments, then you can simply have them follow the same protocol. The reason for this method is that it ensures that you will get paid for your time.

#### *Credit Card Processing Companies*

Some credit card processing companies worth checking out include:

- QuickBooks Intuit
- Your EHRs (which typically has a credit card processor that you can use)
- Square
- PayPal

Before you sign up for any payment-processing companies, read the fine print. Some charge a minimum amount per day, early cancellation fees, and more.

I chose PayPal because we already use it with the business that my husband and I co-founded, and it is a trusted payment method with competitive processing fees. If you do not have a PayPal account, I will walk you through the process of signing up for one now. Please note that you'll need a business checking account before you start this process to have the account verified (and you will want to do so).

*Creating a PayPal Account*

To create a PayPal account:

1. Go to www.paypal.com.

2. Click "Sign Up."

3. Check "Business Account."

4. Select "PayPal Payments Standard."

5. Type in your business email address, enter the code to verify you are not a robot, and click "Next."

6. Follow the prompts to enter your business information.

7. You will be asked if you would like to verify your checking account. Make sure you take this step because it shows your clients the emblem that you are a verified seller.

In the preceding steps, you have done a lot of building. You have crafted your private practice into a legitimate business in the eyes of the state or province and have secured a domain name. You have created your very own logo, built a professional-looking website, and reviewed the pros and cons of a fee-for-service or insurance-based practice. Finally, your business should be ready to accept all payment forms, including credit cards. In the fourth and final step, you will learn how to spread the word that your practice is open for business. We will examine the more traditional ways to market your services, along with exploring some other creative ideas.

# STEP FOUR

# SPREADING THE NEWS!

PART I

# HOW TO REACH YOUR TARGET MARKET

I am really excited for you! The hard parts are behind you, and now you can go out and begin building your presence in the community. You have reached the point where your office is set up and ready to welcome new clients. You have your methods of accepting payments warmed and waiting. Embellished with your fancy logo, your forms are hot off the press and ready to be completed. Now we just need to let your target market know that you exist!

When you are developing your marketing plan, think about how you can improve the community and in what ways your services can be useful. Your goal is to prove to the community leaders that you're an asset to invest in. If you do this part right, I guarantee you'll have their stamp of approval and gain the community's support.

Begin the process with these steps:

- Join the Chamber of Commerce.
- Speak at the local Rotary luncheon meeting.

- Visit schools and churches, asking them where they have observed the greatest need.
- Offer free seminars on topics such as parenting, couples issues, depression, and anxiety at the local schools or churches.
- Visit local business and ask if you can come in and briefly present ways to communicate better with your coworkers at the next staff meeting.
- Ask the area churches if you could volunteer to help out at their next couples' retreat.
- Register to teach a course at the Community Education Center.
- Volunteer for ditch cleanup.
- Sit in on public school meetings; when you hear relevant concerns, call up the people in charge, and tell them how you could make their lives easier.
- Sponsor a local fundraising event.
- Ask to set up a booth outside a major grocery store to raise awareness of mental health disorders. (*Tip: Have a lottery where lucky participants win a $50 gift card that you purchase from the store; this way, those who are leery to come to your booth will venture over, and the store gets business from your gift card purchase. On the entry form, ask if they would like to learn more about your counseling services.*)

- Send an introduction letter to all the major businesses within a 5–10-mile radius of your practice. Make sure you include some marketing materials and a self-addressed, postage-paid return envelope; invite them to send back some materials of their own to cross-promote.
- Order signs from cheapsigns.com and display them at busy intersections. Make sure you check with your local municipality for rules and regulations. Some will have no problem with your signs as long as you abide by the guidelines—others will recommend that you display the signs in a different area.
- Consider marketing by direct mailing.
- Put up flyers around local venues, such as hair salons, gymnastics studios, school bulletin boards, gas stations, churches, grocery stores, coffee shops, etc.
- Host free events.
    - A colleague honored all the business women in her community by hosting an event where the attendees were served wine and appetizers. The local hairdressers styled their hair, and then local photographers took professional photos that were available for purchase online by the business women. This is an example of wonderful networking and a smart marketing idea!
- Ask the local newspaper about a Dear Abby column, and tell the editor that you will write it for free.

- Purchase Google Ads (explained in detail in the next section).
- Put your fancy practice logo across the sides of your vehicle.

Your main focus is to get your private practice name in front of someone in at least three different ways, because on average, it takes three times for someone to see a logo to remember the brand. With your marketing tactics, you want to create a lasting imprint, so that when the times comes that people (or someone they know) need help, your practice logo will come to mind. Think about H&R Block. Once they took their company worldwide and started their new multimedia marketing campaign, they became the first tax company that comes to mind during tax season.

# PART II

# INTRODUCTION TO PAY-PER-CLICK ADVERTISING

## *How to Start Using Google for Paid Advertising*

1. Sign up for a Google My Business account. Before you proceed, Google will tell you that you need to verify that your business actually exists, and then Google will mail you a postcard with a verification code on it. This usually takes about two weeks to arrive at your place of business.

2. When you receive the postcard, enter the verification code where you are told to do so.

3. Now your business is registered in Google maps and will show up on the map when someone searches your private practice by name or service.

4. This action also begins the process of Google looking over your website content and ranking your website based on relevant information. It catalogs the keywords you use so that when a potential client performs a search, your website appears in the search results. It may not (yet) land on the first page, but you can get there; it just takes time.

5. Having your business verified also opens the door to advertise on Google in the form of pay-per-click (PPC) advertising.

6. If you don't have much time to learn the ins and outs of Google ads, simply go to adwordsexpress.com. Put up some fast ads with the help of their support staff who are always waiting to respond to your call, instant message, video chat, or email.

7. If you want to learn more about the specifics of how the ads work, setting ad schedules, and so on, then you will want to visit google.com/adwords. Again, simply ask for assistance, and the support team will virtually hold your hand through the process.

### *Why Would You Consider Paying for Google Ads?*

When potential clients are searching for a therapist or help, they will probably only look at the first page of the search engine results. If your business is new to the scene and has not yet earned it's ranking through Google, you need to pay to get to the front of the line.

When selecting your target audience, be true to your mission statement, as you want your marketing dollars to be spent wisely. Don't put up keywords that don't describe your specialties—just because they are mental health buzzwords.

The PPC advertising can be amazing, yet quite expensive when your settings are not done properly. Make sure you get help from the support team, and keep asking questions until you think that your ads are displaying mainly to those specific populations to whom you are directing your marketing efforts. You'll get the most bang for your buck when you take the time to set up your ads right the first time or fine-tune the settings as necessary.

Great work! You have successfully completed the four steps in opening a private practice. If you followed these steps faithfully, you may now be facing the big question of expanding your practice soon. The following sections include bonus materials that cover expanding your practice, earning passive income, and the importance of paying it forward. Next, I will walk you through the process of determining if expansion is the right decision for your practice, identifying the right time to expand, and exploring various ways to do so.

BONUS MATERIALS

# EXPANDING YOUR PRACTICE, EARNING PASSIVE INCOME, AND PAYING IT FORWARD

PART I

# EXPANDING YOUR PRACTICE

When you reach this point in your business, congratulations! You made it! You were successful at creating a thriving practice, and now you're ready to consider the various options of expanding your brand. When you're considering expanding, it is a perfect time to revisit your mission statement so that it's front and center as you explore the different avenues you can take. Remember, you want your mission statement to be your guide to prevent any mishaps that may land you in the gutter.

## *How Do You Know If Expanding Is the Right Move for You?*

When your practice is operating like a well-oiled machine, you're getting a lot of free publicity, and more and more clients are coming in on a referral basis. You have hit the market and flooded it with your message, so much so that you have doubled or even tripled what you thought your private practice could be over a 1–3-year period. This is how you know that you should consider expanding.

As a business person, you may begin to wonder: *Could I replicate this practice somewhere else? Should I begin offering a greater variety of healing services? Or do I go more mobile and create something online?* These are all very good and appropriate questions. But there is a more important question we must first ask ourselves, the question, "How do you know if expanding is the right move for you?" the answer is, that you know it's the right time to expand when you can see that your practice is as large as it can be and you want more.

At the *initial stage of building your practice*, you should focus on *three core areas of specialization*. Eventually, when you are ready in terms of professional capabilities, and your lifestyle allows it then by all means, consider expanding according to your capacity and personal circumstances.

### *How Do You Know What Exactly to Expand or Add to the Existing Practice?*

Talk to your clients and listen to what they have to say. Ask them what they would like to see if more services were offered. By this time, you have really become involved in the community and have a sense of where there are needs, what would line up with your areas of expertise, and where you would like to grow. Now you can look around the community and within your target market, and find out where the *greatest* needs are. Outline any ideas that you come up with.

A lot of MHPs are keen on the idea of creating an all-inclusive wellness clinic. Let's say your core areas of specialization are couples, adult anxiety, and chronic pain; now you want to add services such as massage therapy, acupuncture, yoga, meditation, and health seminars. Great, now figure out the best strategy to structure the clinic in a way that takes the least amount of your time. If you bring these other healing professionals (HPs) on as employees, you need to manage them. However, if you bring them in by having them sublet space from the practice, you will be able to lease a larger space and then rent out rooms to each of these HPs and simply market their services under your clinic's brand—and at the same time, not be in charge of managing schedules, taking payments, and so on. As you can see, I'm all for creating and automating. I don't want to create a nightmare; to me, if I develop something that excessively consumes my time, then I have betrayed my own personal mission statement.

Another way to expand your practice is by simply opening a second location. To do this, use what you have learned in this book, combined with the personal experience you have gained, and start the process over in a new community. The only thing you don't have to do again is come up with specialty areas and branding; this step is consistent. You should have one or two ICs whom you really trust by now who could head the second location (and then down the road, possibly a third location); let them be the directors of that practice so that you can keep your time and not sign on for more work.

You can also expand simply by upgrading to a bigger office space, and hire additional ICs or remodel your existing space to achieve the desired outcome. If you choose to find another location to expand your practice, make sure you do so with your mission statement by your side. Revisit Step Two: Ideal Life Style and Realistic Budget Planning to ensure that you find the right space that won't pull you in too deeply in terms of CPM.

Maybe you would like a little more freedom and see an opportunity to expand online, with basically zero overhead, and become a life coach or online coach. This is an excellent way to still reach a lot of people who need help and have the ability to work wherever you are—if you go on vacation, need to travel for seminars, or have to take care of a sick kid at home. Online coaching is more motivational than anything, so it allows you to empower others to create the lives they dream of. How rewarding!

### *Why Expand?*

If you have created a replicable model or a scalable practice, you want to expand, because it will give you greater opportunities to earn more passive income. Yes, you create a greater risk; nonetheless, if you are working through the four steps, you are taking much care to reduce any excess risk. I have also heard colleagues say that having multiple practice locations may give you a better chance of being approved for insurance panels, should you opt for that type of practice and that method for expanding.

I understand that not everyone is a business fanatic like I am, but I truly believe that you will instinctively know if expanding is the right option. Now that you have done it once, you won't be as overwhelmed to open a second location or expand. My only warning is to stay true to your lifestyle. Don't create something that will steal your time. Create a business that will free up more time by creating additional income streams.

Until this point, we have discussed how to get your private practice up and running. Now I would like to change gears and explain another topic about which I am passionate—creating passive income. You already started the process when you brought on ICs right away, but let's explore more ways to create products to sell and earn money while you sleep, play with your kids, or sip a daiquiri on the beach.

## PART II

# EARNING PASSIVE INCOME

This section is about creating alternative streams of income in addition to your work as an MHP. It's about guiding you to a place where you can take a week off work and still make money while you're absent. This is the king of all incomes because it doesn't steal your precious time; for this reason, it's called passive income.

What is passive income? It's income that you earn while you are absent; in contrast, direct income is money you earn when you are sitting with a client. If you have a dream to make plenty of money so that you can gain financial freedom, passive income is something you'll need to consider as an MHP. The reason is not due to the nature of our profession; it's because of the way we earn our income. There are only so many hours in a day and a certain number of clients whom we can ethically see in a week. This means that, currently, your earnings are dictated by direct income. To enhance your earnings, you simply need to create a product that you can sell that does not require your direct presence. The following are some examples of passive income:

- Write a book – You have read many books. I bet you could consider yourself knowledgeable in specific areas, so why not write a book, have it edited, and self-publish! Stay tuned for a future book, *How to Generate Passive Income: Simple Steps to Writing a Book.*

- Create a product line – SMC's sister company, B2G, is all about visually reminding people that life can be good again. Specifically, B2G encourages people to reevaluate their goals and priorities, empowering them to make the changes necessary to live a good life. A product line that represents my business brand and mission will allow me to raise awareness of it and create an auxiliary stream of passive income. Stay tuned for a second future book, *Back 2 Good: Simple Steps to Creating a Life Worth Living.*

- Create any kind of product – Your product doesn't have to be therapy related. Read *The 4-Hour Work Week* by Timothy Ferris, who walks you through the entire process of creating passive income and automating the process.

- Create a YouTube channel – If you have something interesting to talk about or to teach, create a YouTube channel. Once your videos receive a certain number of views and subscribers, you will begin to get checks in the mail from YouTube!

### *Why Include Passive Income in the Book?*

I wanted to include passive income in the book because of the monstrosity happening in our culture that tears me up. People are becoming so strapped to their places of employment that when they (or their children) get sick, want to go on vacation, or simply take a day off, they are overcome with stress and panic. They worry that they will get into trouble or that a day off means a day of lost income, affecting their total monthly income. This is a terrible way to live, and I believe that we can do things differently. If this is our one shot at life, why would we not try to open up as much time as we can to play, have fun, and experience all that this life has to offer?

Why do we allow ourselves to think small and be confined by whatever society deems acceptable? You're expected to work hard (really hard) until about the 55–65 age range, and then maybe, if you're lucky, you can retire. If that lines up well (fingers crossed), your health and vitality will be greeting you on the other side of this "work life," and then you'll be ready to explore the world that you have dreamed up for the past 40-some years. Does this seem like a good plan? Take a moment to tally up the number of people around you who have succumbed to premature deaths. How many died by some unforeseeable accident, cancer, or natural causes? I'm sure a lot; every time a person close to retirement dies, what do we always say? "Damn, they were so close to getting to enjoy all the work they put in." Is the loss of life the tragedy, or the fact that they waited 40+ years to live the life they dreamed about? I believe it's the latter; that is why I created B2G, and why I will continue to motivate others to do things differently and enjoy life now. In my opinion, waiting to live is more foolish than playing a game of Russian roulette.

As you can see, I feel very strongly about guiding you in a direction where it's possible to generate passive income. I have had a front-row seat, watching death sneak in and steal a soul on the verge of playtime; it simply breaks my heart when people wait until life is 60% over (if we're lucky) to do the things they enjoy most. I want more for you, and by now I know you do too.

We are winding down on our journey together, with only one more section to go. In the remaining pages, I'm going to address how you should handle the extra attention your success will bring you. What do I mean by this? When you open a new practice that thrives, other MHPs notice. You will be emailed (many times) and asked to join one of your "competitors" for a cup of coffee just to *chat*, a.k.a., *"Tell me how the hell you are so successful, PLEASE!"* In the end, I hope to change your perception of the competition as a threat to a perception of them as simply other MHPs whom you can help.

# PART III

# PAYING IT FORWARD

Quoting the great words of Alan Davis, "There will always be competition, and there will always be plenty to go around. Simply do good work, and you will be fine."

I feel sometimes that we experience the threat of scarcity too intensely in our culture, so much so that we choose not to help fellow MHPs for fear they will come and steal our clients. This could be true, but it's a minuscule concern when you take a look at the bigger picture. In the grand scheme of things, who do you think would end up on top—the ones who kept all the secrets for success to themselves and got rich, or those who found simple ways to earn a good living and shared their ideas with the world? When you put good stuff out into the world with a pure intention, it will return to you again and again. Don't lose sight of why we are here because of a perceived threat or the feeling of scarcity. Help one another; there is enough to go around for all of us.

Trust me, when colleagues notice your success, they will come knocking. Take this as a compliment, not as a threat. Think of how much courage it takes for them to approach you in the first place, especially if the MHPs are senior practitioners and asking a newbie to help guide their own (established) practice. Help them; remember that karma is a wonderful thing, and you just got it on your side.

Now don't get me wrong; I'm not asking you to be a saint and forget all business sense when it comes to being smart about whom you aid or don't aid. Obviously, I won't advise you to help your direct competitors to get more clients. I'm simply reminding you that others will want to pick your brain for ideas to help their private practice survive. Give them a piece of your time and support.

I believe that paying it forward has largely contributed to my success. I have helped several MHPs gain the courage to open new practices and strengthen existing ones. Do I do all these for free? No. I did in the beginning, but now I have managed to distinguish what amount of time to give away and what to charge for. I can meet with them and talk in general about some changes they could make, but when it comes to restructuring their practice and developing an individualized plan, I am hired as a consultant. As previously discussed, our time here is precious, so be careful how you spend it. This way you won't feel like you are betraying your lifestyle, and you will demonstrate or (as we say in therapy) "model" how to value your time.

We are in the helping profession, so let's help everyone, not only those who pay for it. Don't do the work for them—that will only prolong failure; instead, teach them how to do it right, so they learn for long-term success. Who knows, maybe at some point, you will be like me and get hired as a business consultant. Never forget the big picture in life; to reiterate, when you put good stuff out, good stuff will come back.

# CLOSING THOUGHTS

Wow, that's it! I can't believe we made it to the end already. I hope you have enjoyed this book and can see how simple it truly is to build your own practice and double your paycheck. A lot of things in life are legitimately scary, but don't let a business decision be one of those. If you do your research and follow the four simple steps, you will be well on your way to building a successful practice and living a life of which you have dreamed for so long.

Good luck! If you need help with resources or have additional questions, you can reach me directly at Jessica@southmetrocounseling.com. To ensure that your email does not get overlooked or go to my spam folder, please put "Private Practice Question" in the Subject line.

Thank you, and I wish you the greatest success in everything you do,
Jessica M. Miller, M.A.

# FOR FURTHER READING

**Books**

Ferris, T. *The 4-Hour Work Week*. New York: Crown Publishing Group, 2009.

**Therapist Directory**

Psychology Today – http://www.psychologytoday.com

**Graphic Designers and Other Freelance Work**

Elance – http://www.elance.com

**Secretary of State**

Minnesota – http://www.sos.state.mn.us

**Internal Revenue Service**

FEIN – https://sa.www4.irs.gov/modiein/individual/index.jsp

(800) 829-4933

**Marketing Material/Business Cards**

Vistaprint – https://www.vistaprint.com

**Web Design Platforms**

Squarespace – http://www.squarespace.com

Weebly – http://www.weebly.com

Wix – http://www.wix.com

**Photo Resale Sites**

123rf – http://www.123rf.com

Getty Images – http://www.gettyimages.com

iStock – http://www.istock.com

Shutter Stock – http://www.shutterstock.com

**Payment Platforms**

PayPal – http://www.paypal.com

QuickBooks Intuit – http://quickbooks.intuit.com

Square – http://www.square.com

**Marketing Websites**

Google AdWords – https://www.google.com/adwords/

CPSIA information can be obtained
at www.ICGtesting.com
Printed in the USA
FFOW04n1835151115
18530FF

9 780996 309301